Unlimited Partnership

God and the Businessman

Bob Yandian

Bob Yandian Ministries
Tulsa, Oklahoma

bobyandian.com

UNLIMITED PARTNERSHIP
GOD AND THE BUSINESSMAN
ISBN 1-885600-01-1
© 1996 by Bob Yandian
Bob Yandian Ministries
P.O. Box 55236
Tulsa, Oklahoma 74155-1236

Published by Bob Yandian Ministries
P.O. Box 55236
Tulsa, Oklahoma 74155-1236

Contents

One very important
ingredient of success
is a good, wide-awake,
persistent, tireless enemy.

— Unknown

A Business That Cannot Fail

How would you like to go into business with God? With a partner who is all powerful, who knows the past and the future, and who has perfect wisdom for every occasion, there would be no limit to your potential!

Such a partnership with God is what I call an *"unlimited partnership."* Today, God is calling many men and women into just such a partnership.

In fact, there is as much of a calling into *business* as there is into a pulpit ministry. Both are of equal importance in God's overall plan. In the Old Testament, Moses told his people that it was God who gave them the ability to create wealth to establish His covenant (Deuteronomy 8:18).

God has not changed in the New Testament. He

still gives talents and spiritual power to generate wealth in this fallen world. The purpose of wealth in the New Testament remains the same as in the Old: *"...to establish His covenant."* A businessman or woman is called by God to financially support those who preach the gospel.

> ## THE PURPOSE OF WEALTH IN THE NEW TESTAMENT REMAINS THE SAME AS IN THE OLD: *"...TO ESTABLISH HIS COVENANT."*

So if God has called you into business, don't quit to go into mission work or evangelism because somebody makes you feel inferior to those in the full-time pulpit ministry. The businessman who tries to be a preacher is as bad as the preacher who tries to be a businessman! Businessmen or women should stay with their divine call to make a profit, expand their business, and finance the gospel.

A SPIRITUAL ARMY

In these last days, the Lord is raising up a mighty, spiritual army of missionaries, evangelists, pastors, and teachers. There must be funds to support them.

Soldiers have always been supported by public funds. David, speaking prophetically, said the men who went into battle would be rewarded equally with those who remained behind to *"stay by the stuff"* (I Samuel 30:24). In God's eyes, too, those who *"stay by the stuff"* are equally important as those who go to battle. At the judgment seat of Christ, the business owners and employees in the congregation who remained in everyday life and generated capital to support the gospel will be given equal rewards with those who stood behind the pulpits in this country and around the world. Like David, God rewards equally.

GOD LOVES BUSINESS

It may come as a surprise to you, but it's true: *God loves business.* It is His means of producing wealth in the earth. Governments cannot produce wealth and neither can churches. They can only distribute it. Business is the only place where wealth can be created. When a government understands this and frees business to operate with only minimal restraint, great amounts of wealth and prosperity come into a nation.

Likewise, when the Church sees God's purpose for business and does not condemn its members for possessing great wealth or owning powerful businesses, it, too, can see large amounts of wealth and prosperity brought in. To bless businesses and honor those in business is to honor God and His divine will. His plan for taking the gospel to the ends of the earth has business at its core.

Business did not begin with Wall Street or Dow Jones. Henry Ford and J. Paul Getty might have taken business to new heights, but they weren't the first businessmen in history. When only one man occupied the earth, there was business. Adam was the first businessman, but even *he* did not create business: God did. God and Adam formed the first business partnership.

Even after Satan tempted Eve in the Garden and man fell, God was still Adam's business partner. God never left His original intention: *Business was to be a vehicle for the message of redemption to be taken into the world.* When men and women, Old Testament and New, put the Lord and His plan first in their lives, God prospered them financially. He blessed all that they set their hand to (Deuteronomy 28:8).

OVERCOMING RESISTANCE

One change did occur because of Adam's sin, however. A curse entered into business. God told Adam, *"Cursed is the ground for thy sake"* (Genesis 3:17).

Adam's business was agriculture, the working of the ground. As the Lord God spoke these words, a curse came against business, and it has continued from that day forward.

Agriculture has been and still is the basis for all business, because, in a way, all business comes from the earth. The earth continually produces plants and animals and renews the air and water. Genesis 8:22 tells us, *"While the earth remaineth... seedtime and harvest...shall not cease."* All metals, fuels, wood, paper, plastic, food or drinks come from the ground. Even our modern "stock markets" began with farmers and ranchers bringing their products together to barter and trade among themselves.

Mankind and business are inseparably linked together because man also comes from the dust of the ground. When a person enters a profession which he really enjoys, it's as if he becomes a part of the business and the business becomes a part of him. We give life to the business and the business gives life to us. God designed business to be a source of pleasure and fulfillment as well as a source of income. Because of this, many times we have to put safeguards on ourselves so we do not become workaholics, consumed by our work.

MANKIND AND BUSINESS ARE INSEPARABLY LINKED TOGETHER BECAUSE MAN ALSO COMES FROM THE DUST OF THE GROUND.

When the earth was cursed, thorns and weeds entered the ground and Adam's business met resistance. God now told Adam:

Genesis 3:17,19:

> *...in sorrow [under great pressure] shalt thou eat of it [the ground]...In the sweat of thy face shalt thou eat bread, till thou return unto the ground.*

Until now, Adam had never raised a sweat working in the Garden. Everything Adam did met with instant success. Now, however, his success would come through much hard work. Yet, God did not tell Adam to give up. He did not tell him the thorns and weeds were greater than his best effort. No resistance is ever greater than God's blessing.

There is an enemy, it's true. He is wide-awake, persistent, and tireless, but his plans against us will never succeed.

Although business meets with resistance and hardship, God's promise of success is greater than any curse of Satan or the world.

God wants to form an unlimited partnership with you, a partnership greater than hell itself. Jesus promised protection for His Church and said, *"...the gates of hell shall not prevail against it"* (Matthew 16:18).

When a Christian man or woman operates their business on godly, biblical principles, it will face opposition, but that business cannot fail.

The only difference between businesses is how they take care of customers.
— Unknown

The Heart of Your Unlimited Partner

Pastoring a church has given me a tremendous appreciation for the businessman. I am so thankful to God for the many business owners and employees who attend our church and faithfully give their tithes and offerings. Without their support, the church could not be a success.

Pastoring has also given me compassion for businessmen and women. I understand the challenges they face. Although a church is not a business, there are many aspects of business found within its day-to-day activities. As a pastor, I am accountable over these areas just as a business owner or manager would be. Finances have to be in order, profits from sales and fund-raisers have to be counted and deposited, and designated offerings have to be put into the proper accounts.

Plans for the future must be made, buildings have to be constructed and paid for. The pressure on the leaders and decision makers can be intense!

Dealing with these same issues as a pastor has given me great insight into the businessman's calling in God's kingdom. I can see that the heart of God for a business is no different than the heart of God for a church. *I'm convinced that if you find the heart of God and make it your heart also, you can only succeed!*

FINDING GOD'S HEART

I've discovered a key question to help find God's heart for your business. It is: "Who pays the bills?" Knowing this keep things in perspective. In operating either a church or a business, it is easy to get caught up in the everyday activities and forget who pays the bills.

I'M CONVINCED THAT IF YOU FIND
THE HEART OF GOD AND MAKE
IT YOUR HEART ALSO, YOU CAN
ONLY SUCCEED!

As an employee, it is easy to get your eyes on the owner, the manager, or the payroll officer. You assume he is the one you need to please, because he signs your check. However, the one who signs the checks is not the one who pays the bills. There is a difference. To succeed, you must serve the one who pays the bills!

ROW, ROW, ROW

There is a little fragment of a verse in Acts which has stuck with me and helped me through the years whenever I have forgotten who really holds the power in my church. Its application into business is invaluable.

Acts 13:5b reads, *"... they had also John to their minister."* This verse was written about Paul and Barnabas who were just starting out on their first missionary journey. They took John Mark with them, the young man who wrote the book of Mark. The key to understanding this verse is the word "minister." It is not the usual word for minister, but the Greek word *huperetes*. Seldom appearing in the New Testament, it is a compound word meaning *an underrower.*

In the ancient world, the large ships were powered by hundreds of slaves, who rowed on three levels. The newest slaves were placed on the bottom level where the work was the hardest. Their oars dipped deeper into the water and required more effort to row. As you gained more time aboard the ship, it was considered a promotion to be sent to a higher level. Of course, the most envied position for a slave was to be on the top level of rowers.

John Mark, a young man new in the ministry, began his spiritual responsibility as an underrower with two veterans, Paul and Barnabas. John Mark's work load was much greater than theirs, and he probably griped as they ate and fellowshipped with other ministers while he had to book hotel rooms and help set up chairs for the meetings.

At first, he was probably excited about the glamour of travel. Later, however, as he discovered a price had to be paid before he could "row on the top level" with Paul and Barnabas, he got discouraged and quit. Acts 13:13 tells us, *"...and*

John departing from them returned to Jerusalem."

I have seen the same scenario happen again and again in churches, ministries, and businesses. Talented and anointed people lose their perspective, get discouraged, and quit.

LOOK ONE MORE LEVEL UP

In cases like this, I just want to cry out, "Wait a minute! Don't lose sight of what we're here for! Paul may be a top-level rower, but don't forget: *there is a deck on this ship."* Someone rides up there. They are the paying customers. They make it possible for the ship to exist and operate. They're why we do what we do. They're who we are here to serve – not the top-level rowers.

How quickly we forget! The boss may sign the check, but it's the customers who make it possible to have money in the checking account. The boss may be important, but he is still a rower. The customer pays the bills.

My wife and I have enjoyed being on a few cruises. The ship's crew is there all week long to serve your every need. They stand ready to entertain you with onboard spas, fully equipped gyms, poolside service, and a wide variety of daytime and evening activities.

One of the highlights of each night is when the ship's captain comes to your dinner table and speaks with you. You think, "What a privilege to meet the captain of such a large ship." NO! What a privilege it is for the captain to meet the paying customers. *They* make his job possible. The captain is still a rower.

THE CUSTOMER IS TOPS!

There are some department stores I try to avoid. I have walked into them on many occasions and could not get anyone to wait on me. When someone finally did, they acted like I should consider it a privilege that they took time away from their other duties to help me. After all, they were counting the money in their till, pricing the new fall line, or meeting with their supervisor. They made it clear: Customers were toward the bottom of their list of priorities.

But wait! The customer is the one who makes it possible to have money to put in the till. He generates the revenue for the fall line to be ordered and the capital to pay the supervisor. Not to mention that without the customer, even the snobbish salesperson would not have a job!

There is an endless list in America of companies who have gone bankrupt because they became too big and arrogant to care for people. Other large companies are facing downsizing because they are being surpassed by fast-growing companies that put the customer back into their rightful position — on top, back on the deck of the ship.

> THERE IS AN ENDLESS LIST IN AMERICA OF COMPANIES WHO HAVE GONE BANKRUPT BECAUSE THEY BECAME TOO BIG AND ARROGANT TO CARE FOR PEOPLE.

The growing businesses today that seem to be unaffected by the ups and downs of the marketplace are those that believe *the customer is always right.*

One such example is the Nordstrom Department Stores.

When Nordstrom stores began, a meeting was held with the first employees. They were told, "Value the customer above everything else. If a customer wants a refund for something and does not have a receipt or a box, give them the refund. If a customer rolls a tire down the aisle and wants a refund, give them their money back."

At this point, a salesperson spoke up and said, "But, sir, we do not sell tires."

The manager reiterated, "I said, give them their money back."

A few customers may take advantage of these policies and a loss will be suffered, but the vast majority will make that business a part of their lives for many years to come. The odds are always in your favor when you put people first.

Every business has customers, whether it is sales to other companies or selling directly to consumers. You may be involved in manufacturing, distributing, or retailing, but without customers, your company would cease to exist. Not only does upper management need to recognize this, but all the other employees must see it, too. You are all rowers.

PEOPLE AND YOUR
UNLIMITED PARTNER

When you mention people, you have the ear of your Unlimited Partner. *God loves people.* He sent His own Son to the Cross for people. He did not send redemption for anything else in creation — only for people. He left us here on the earth after we were saved for one purpose: *People.* The Great Commission, the gifts of the Holy Spirit, and the local church with its many programs are all tools God has given us to bless people.

When you see your business in the same light, you will begin to unleash the power of your Unlimited Partner. The power of any business is in its vision. The vision of God is people. When you have His vision, you can do nothing else but succeed.

Set your business focus on taking care of people

and their needs, and money will follow. When Abraham went after his family who were taken captive by the five wicked kings, he came back not only with his loved ones, but also with a great amount of wealth (Genesis 14). The same happened with David at Ziklag. He went with a small army to bring back the wives and children, but he also came back with more money than he could use (I Samuel 30).

SET YOUR BUSINESS FOCUS ON TAKING CARE OF PEOPLE AND THEIR NEEDS, AND MONEY WILL FOLLOW.

Jesus did not go into Satan's domain to redeem money. *He went for people* and brought back material spoils, too (Isaiah 53:12).

If you seek to meet the needs of the customer (the people), God will see to it that profits will come and your company will grow strong. If you will put people on the deck of the ship, you will have the same priorities God has. You will be seeking first the kingdom of God and His righteousness. God then promises you "*..all these things shall be added unto you*" (Matthew 6:33).

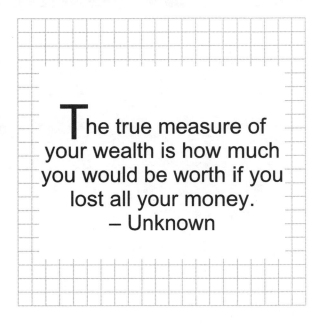

The true measure of your wealth is how much you would be worth if you lost all your money.
– Unknown

CHAPTER THREE

God's Purpose For Making Money

In Luke's Gospel, Jesus tells us, *"...the children of this world are in their generation wiser than the children of light"* (Luke 16:8).

Many believers have read this verse and wondered, "What would prompt Jesus to make such a hard statement concerning the children of God?" This passage is from a parable Jesus taught about an unjust steward. Jesus used this parable to teach us how to handle money.

THE UNJUST STEWARD

This parable is not meant to be a comparison to the Christian life, but a contrast. If the evil and wicked sinners of this earth know how to prepare a future for themselves with money, Christians should be as wise and even wiser. Yet, in this parable Jesus is saying children of the world are wiser than believers.

I have discovered this to be the case in our day as well. Many Christians have no insurance, no retirement fund, and no savings account. They refuse to lay up for the future — all in the name of "Jesus is coming soon." This is not wisdom, it's foolishness.

I Timothy 5:8

> If any provide not for his own, and specially for those of his own house [family], he hath denied the faith [the Word], and is worse than an infidel.

Only a Christian can be worse than an infidel. Even sinners know they should provide money and a financial future for their own family.

When a Christian knows how to use the money of this world to prepare a future for himself and his family, he is equally as wise as the world. But the point of this parable is not for us to be just as wise as the world, but even wiser.

HOW TO BECOME WISER
THAN THE WORLD

Jesus told us there is a higher usage of money than simply preparing for this natural life. Although retirement, savings, and insurance are all wise, there is something wiser.

Luke 16:9

> *Make to yourselves friends [converts] of the mammon of unrighteousness [money of the world]; that [so], when ye fail [die], they may receive you into everlasting habitations.*

Money given into the gospel will win souls. Converts for Jesus make true friends which will last for all eternity.

As good as a retirement fund or savings account may be, they are only good for this lifetime. Your savings, mutual funds, or I.R.A.s will not be there to greet you in the kingdom of heaven. Only those whose lives you affect for the Lord will be in heaven. They will not only greet you, but be with you for all eternity!

The wisest investment any believer can make is an investment into the kingdom of God. *The highest priority of life is eternal life.*

THE WISEST INVESTMENT ANY BELIEVER CAN MAKE IS AN INVESTMENT INTO THE KINGDOM OF GOD.

THE GREATER RICHES

Luke 16:11:

> *If therefore ye have not been faithful in the unrighteous mammon, who will commit to your trust the true riches?*

This is a powerful statement. The wise use of money will bring God's trust for greater riches. What are the greater riches? The greater riches are revelation of the promises of God's Word.

Proverbs 3:13-15:

> *Happy is the man that findeth wisdom, and the man that getteth understanding.*
>
> *For the merchandise [profit] of it [wisdom]*

*is better than the merchandise of silver,
and the gain thereof than fine gold.*

*She [wisdom] is more precious than rubies:
and all the things thou canst desire are not
to be compared unto her.*

I hope you understand the impact of Jesus' statement. When a person's highest priority in life is to sow into God's kingdom, win souls, and disciple Christians, the Holy Spirit is under divine order and obligation to reveal more of God's Word, the true riches, to that believer.

If, on the other hand, someone is not faithful with the world's money and does not make giving into God's kingdom their greatest priority, God is under no obligation to give them more revelation and understanding of His Word. The greater riches are entrusted to those with the greater wisdom.

DO YOU WANT A GREATER YEAR?

This can become a year to remember. Why not make this the greatest year of your personal life and of your business?

Surpass the world in wisdom. Make giving of your tithes and offerings from your personal and business income into God's kingdom a higher priority than anything else in your life. Allow your Unlimited Partner to not only bring wealth into your business, but also let Him *direct* the money.

ALLOW YOUR UNLIMITED PARTNER TO NOT ONLY BRING WEALTH INTO YOUR BUSINESS, BUT ALSO LET HIM *DIRECT* THE MONEY

Your riches will increase in this life and will also remain throughout the ages to come. Your insight into the Word of God will increase and you will gain friends (converts) with the world's money. Those souls which were won through your giving will welcome you into heaven for all eternity.

No other investment plan can compare with God's plan, because the world has no wisdom that compares to God's wisdom!

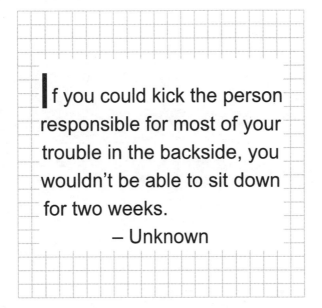

If you could kick the person responsible for most of your trouble in the backside, you wouldn't be able to sit down for two weeks.

– Unknown

Business On The Front Lines

One of the greatest admonitions to business owners is found in the following passage:

James 4:13-17

Go to [come on] now, ye that say, To day or to morrow we will go into such a city, and continue there a year, and buy and sell, and get gain [make profit]:

Whereas ye know not what shall be on the morrow. For what is your life? It is even a vapour, that appeareth for a little time, and then vanisheth away.

For that [but] ye ought to say, If the Lord will, we shall live [continue], and do this, or that.

But now [as it is] ye rejoice in your boastings

[braggings]: all such rejoicing is evil.

Therefore to him that knoweth to do good,
and doeth it not, to him it is sin.

James was the pastor of a church in Jerusalem just before the fall of that great religious and economic center. The church James pastored was filled with some of the wealthiest business people in the ancient world. These were primarily Jews who had been born again. Some were already in business when they received Jesus while others began their business ventures after their salvation.

THE VOICE OF THEIR PASTOR

Many consider the two books of Timothy and the book of Titus to be the only pastoral books of the New Testament. These books were written by Paul to pastors of churches. However, the epistle of James is the only New Testament book written by a pastor to his congregation. I consider it to be the greatest, though most overlooked, book of admonition to the local church.

To be a member of James' church was a great honor. James was the brother of the Lord Jesus (Matthew 13:55), although he was not converted until after the Resurrection. His sermons were probably filled with great stories from his childhood of seeing the Lord Jesus grow up right in his own home. He could also strongly preach that salvation does not come because we grow up in a Christian home or even by having Jesus as a part of our family. James was living proof that every individual must personally receive Jesus as Lord and Savior for himself.

Because James' church was located in Jerusalem, many of the great ministers were present each week for services. It was possible to look down the rows of seats and see Peter, John, or even the Apostle Paul if he was home from one of his many missionary trips.

Wonderful missions conferences were held in Jerusalem. When the Gentiles first received the Holy Spirit, it was announced at James' church. Later, the speakers hotly debated whether the Gentiles needed to be circumcised or keep any other part of the Law of Moses.

There was always something happening at the church in Jerusalem. It set precedents for all the other churches in the known world.

However, James was not as thrilled with his congregation as they were with him. As James looked over this large group of people each week, he saw arrogance creeping into their hearts. Church was no longer a place to worship the Lord: it had become a place for believers to show off their new wealth and to compete for favored seating in the sanctuary.

Although the Word was being taught, it no longer meant as much to the people. Church had become a place to make a social statement rather than a place to see people's lives changed, healed, and stabilized through the Word of God. Those who did not have a high social status were being seated in the back of the church, and the wealthy were given places of high visibility. The poor of the church and the city were being overlooked. Hypocrisy was rampant.

CHURCH HAD BECOME A PLACE
TO MAKE A SOCIAL STATEMENT
RATHER THAN A PLACE TO SEE
PEOPLE'S LIVES CHANGED,
HEALED, AND STABILIZED
THROUGH THE WORD OF GOD.

James 2:2-4

> *For if there come unto your assembly a man with a gold ring, in goodly apparel, and ther come in also a poor man in vile rainment;*

> *And ye have respect to him that weareth the gay clothing, and say unto him, Sit thou here in a good place; and say to the poor, Stand thou there, or sit here under my footstool:*

> *Are ye not then partial in yourselves, and are become judges of evil thoughts?*

The Lord was given lip service during church, but the same tongues were gossiping, back-biting, and maligning others after church (James 3:8–11). The church had begun with a genuine outpouring of the Holy Spirit (Acts 2:1-4), but the love of money had replaced the love of the Lord.

BUSINESS AS USUAL?

One group which James addressed harshly was the business people of his congregation. James had watched them begin their businesses with a love for souls, the Lord, and the local church. Their hearts were pure, and each business decision had been started with prayer. God was their senior business partner, and they prospered in their ventures from the very beginning.

They had realized the important link between business and the local church. Their talent to generate money was God-given, and they walked in the spiritual office of a giver (Romans 12:8) just as James walked in the spiritual office of pastor (Ephesians 4:11).

But now their hearts had changed. They no longer entered business decisions with prayer and thanksgiving. Gratitude to the Lord was the last thing on their mind. They began to think *they* had caused their business to prosper. The Holy Spirit was forgotten, and the people started to rely on business forecasters and market analysts to plan their future expansions. Their business capital was so tied up they could not give into the church. They had lost the true perspective on godly business and prosperity. God was their partner in name only and was no longer consulted. They had now become a *limited partnership.*

Their business perspective used to be to further the eternal kingdom, but now they only thought of blessing their own temporary lives. James reminds the congregation that the kingdom of God is eternal, but their life is momentary by comparison. The life of the most powerful business tycoon is as brief as that of the most insignificant manual laborer. All of us have a life that is *"but a vapour."* Like a puff of steam, we are here for a few moments, and then we step into eternity.

STANDING AT THE BORDER

Business owners and Christian businesses stand

at the border between the Church and the world. They are positioned at the gates of God's kingdom. Business men and women form a bridge to bring the money from the world's system into the kingdom of God. This money is used by the local church to win the lost, help support evangelists and missionaries, and bring maturity to the saints of God. There is no limit to the amount of success and wealth God wants to bring to a business when those in charge understand their role in God's endtime plan.

> ## BUSINESS MEN AND WOMEN FORM A BRIDGE TO BRING THE MONEY FROM THE WORLD'S SYSTEM INTO THE KINGDOM OF GOD.

The Apostle Paul gave Timothy some guidelines for Christian businessmen who stand on the border between the Church and the world:

1 Timothy 6:17,18:

> *Charge them that are rich in this world, that they be not highminded, nor trust in uncertain riches, but in the living God, who*

giveth us richly all things to enjoy;

That they do good, that they be rich in good works [honorable production], *ready to distribute* [to the poor], *willing to communicate* [give tithes and offerings].

Timothy was the pastor at Ephesus, which, like Jerusalem, was also a large business city. But while Jerusalem was a haven for Jewish business leaders, Ephesus had mainly Gentile entrepreneurs. Those in Timothy's church were born again just like the Jewish business people in James' church. The same temptations face all redeemed business owners. There is a great pull to trust in new-found riches and not in the Lord.

Paul instructed Timothy to remind these zealous business people to keep their priorities straight and not lose their original godly vision. God blesses all of us so we may be able to bless the kingdom of God. Money is to be used for *"good works."* This is giving to the poor and funding the work of the local church. Our temporary and brief life's purpose is to fund the eternal kingdom of God. Our works for the Lord will endure for both time and *eternity.*

The admonitions of James and Paul to those in business still hold true today. After two thousand years, business is still designed by God to bless the individual with good things to be enjoyed as well as to bless the kingdom of God.

Should Jesus not return in the next few years, business will continue for centuries to come. Principles for successful Christian businesses will be the same then as they are today. *Business success in any century begins by accepting the plan of God.*

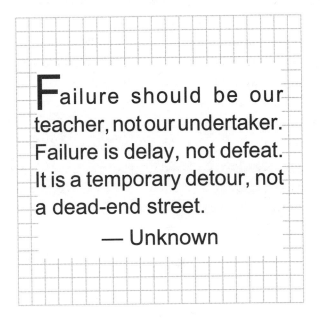

Failure should be our teacher, not our undertaker. Failure is delay, not defeat. It is a temporary detour, not a dead-end street.

— Unknown

No More Monkey Business

In the book of Deuteronomy, Moses gives his final discourse to the children of Israel just before they enter the Promised Land. He tells them why he won't be going with them.

Deuteronomy 3:23-27

And I besought the Lord att that time, saying,

O Lord God, thou hast begun to show thy servant thy greatness, and thy mighty hand: for what God is there in heaven or in earth, that can do according to thy works, and according to thy might?

I pray thee, let me go over, and see the good land that is beyond Jordan, that goodly mountain, and Lebanon.

But the Lord was wroth with me for your sakes, and would not hear me: and the Lord said unto me, Let it suffice thee; speak no more unto me of this matter.

Get thee up into the top of Pisgah, and lift up thine eyes westward, and northward, and southward, and eastward, and behold it with thine eyes: for thou shalt not go over this Jordan.

Moses then recounts the many things they must remember. In Chapter 8, he warns the children of Israel not to forget God once they become prosperous in their new homeland.

Deuteronomy 8:10,11:

When thou hast eaten and art full, then thou shalt bless the Lord thy God for the good land which he hath given thee.

Beware that thou forget not the Lord thy God, in not keeping his commandments, and his judgments, and his statutes, which I command thee this day.

Despite Moses' warning, Israel *did forget* the Lord.

Once they entered the Promised Land, planted their crops, moved into nice homes, and gained wealth, they began to brag on themselves. They thought their own wisdom and talents obtained the land and overcame their enemies. This opened the door for many invasions in the days ahead and eventual domination by the Philistines.

That same chapter in Deuteronomy tells what must be done to maintain wealth and blessings:

Deuteronomy 8:18

> *But thou shalt remember the Lord thy God: for it is he that giveth thee power* [ability] *to get wealth, that he may establish his covenant which he sware unto thy fathers, as it is this day.*

This is a key verse to Christian businessmen in every generation. God is telling those who desire to find great wealth that they must come back to their foundations of trusting in God *daily.* Each day must begin and end with thanksgiving to God for His power in us to obtain wealth. The profits must also be given to win the lost so God's covenant can continue to be spread in the earth.

GOD IS TELLING THOSE WHO
DESIRE TO FIND GREAT WEALTH
THAT THEY MUST COME BACK
TO THEIR FOUNDATIONS OF
TRUSTING IN GOD *DAILY*. EACH
DAY MUST BEGIN AND END WITH
THANKSGIVING TO GOD...

TIMES REALLY HAVEN'T CHANGED

Fifteen centuries later, the early Christian businessmen in James' congregation made the same mistake as the children of Israel: *They forgot to acknowledge the Lord in their businesses.* They began to think their own talents and abilities had produced this newly acquired wealth. Having begun the race with their eyes on the Lord, they soon began to look at themselves. They forgot to consult the Lord as they had done when their business first began. Although they still considered God to be their business partner, they never asked Him for advice.

These men knew what to do, but were not doing it (James 4:17). Let's look at some of the pitfalls these businessmen fell into. If we study their mistakes, we can avoid making the same ones in our day, because times really have not changed.

1. They made business decisions without consulting the Lord.

James 4:13

For that ye ought to say, If the Lord will, we shall live, and do this, or that.

These business leaders said they would visit *"such and such a city and continue there a year."* They believed the economy of certain areas was better than others, and they made the decisions to commit to that city the finances and time to establish another business division or franchise. They thought it would take about a year and that the risk would be well worth it. All of this is perfectly within the will of God, but they forgot one thing: *consulting the Holy Spirit.*

A healthy economy today may not be so

tomorrow. In an unstable economy, you cannot predict what tomorrow may bring. You may be thinking, "But risk is just a part of business." This might be true for the world, but not for the believer. The Holy Spirit knows *exactly* what will happen to the economy tomorrow, next week, and next year.

THE HOLY SPIRIT KNOWS EXACTLY WHAT WILL HAPPEN TO THE ECONOMY TOMORROW, NEXT WEEK, AND NEXT YEAR.

Remember, God wants to be your business partner. His knowledge is unlimited. He sees the future better than we see the present. As you pray over each new venture and business decision, it pulls your Unlimited Partner back to the table of the board room and draws from His omniscience.

2. They wanted to make a profit for themselves and not for the Lord.

James 4:13

> *Go to now, ye that say, Today or tomorrow*
> *we will go into such a city, and continue a*
> *year, and buy and sell, and get gain.*

The motive for business switched from a means of promoting the gospel to a means of producing more income. Money is not evil, and profit in business is legitimate with God, but covetousness is never acceptable with the Lord (Hebrews 13:5). Money is not the root of all evil, but the *love* of it (1 Timothy 6:10).

Every business deal should be seen as another opportunity to help spread the gospel. Firstfruits giving does not apply to personal income alone, but also for businesses. Just as God blesses us personally for giving into the gospel, He also blesses our business as we give into His kingdom.

3. They began to feel invincible.

James 4:14

> *Whereas ye know not what shall be on the*
> *morrow. For what is your life? It is even a*

*vapour, that appeareth for a little time, and
then vanisheth away.*

Like the Israelites of old, these business
owners began to say, "My power and the
might of mine hand hath gotten me this
wealth." James reminds them that they are
not immortal and like everyone else, their life
is like a vapor of steam which appears for
a moment and then vanishes. Their life on
earth is brief compared to eternity!

Whether rich or poor, company president
or janitor, every believer must die and
stand before the judgment seat of Christ
(2 Corinthians 5:10). This life we have and
the talents we possess are to be used for the
Lord Jesus and the promotion of His kingdom.
God's instructions in Deuteronomy were true
in James' day — and are still true in ours.

4.   They neglected daily communion with God

James 4:15

*For that ye ought to say, If the Lord will,
we shall live, and do this, or that.*

The men who began their companies with daily fellowship with God eventually forgot Him. They did not stop to remember the many critical times the Holy Spirit warned them concerning opportunities that looked good to the eye, but were not. Other times, God's Spirit gave them a "go ahead" about opportunities that most people would have rejected, but later proved successful.

Oh, the infinite wisdom and understanding of the Holy Spirit who has been sent to be our Guide! Whether we are businessmen or common laborers, we should never forget the One who can see into the future. He is never bound by man's economy or stock averages. The Holy Spirit receives His wisdom from God the Father and supplies everything for us from God's eternal riches in heaven (Philippians 4:19).

5. They became arrogant.

James 4:16

But now ye rejoice in your boastings: all such rejoicing is evil.

Where they used to be boasting about the goodness of the Lord, these business people were now bragging about their own wisdom and business abilities. God not only gave us talents to glorify Him, but our breath was also given to praise Him (Psalm 150:6).

James tells the business people in his congregation that their arrogant boastings and braggings are evil. When we are consumed with the Lord, our mouth will speak of Him. When we are consumed with our own abilities, our mouth will speak of ourselves. Jesus said, *"Out of the abundance of the heart the mouth speaketh"* (Matthew 12:34).

WHEN WE ARE CONSUMED WITH THE LORD, OUR MOUTH WILL SPEAK OF HIM. WHEN WE ARE CONSUMED WITH OUR OWN ABILITIES, OUR MOUTH WILL SPEAK OF OURSELVES.

6. They knew what to do to ensure their future but were not doing it.

James 4:17

Therefore to him that knoweth to do good,
and doeth it not, to him it is sin.

James tells them they are sinning because they knew what to do and were not doing it. He is not telling them something they do not know! They were well aware they were sinning but were too wrapped up in their present success to look to God's answer. Their attitude was, "If it isn't broke, why fix it?"

Things were presently going well for them because of the good crop they had sown years before. However, James is warning them that they were now sowing self-destruction into their businesses. In a short time, these seeds would grow, and the business which had been so greatly prospered would take a downturn. James is merely confirming what their own hearts and the Holy Spirit had been telling them for a long time.

Approximately twenty years after James wrote

this epistle, the great city of Jerusalem fell to the Romans. Those businessmen who had sought for and obeyed the advice of their Unlimited Partner had moved their businesses elsewhere before the city was beseiged and destroyed. Those who relied on their own wisdom and stayed, lost all they had.

The Lord is so good to let us know well in advance that destruction is on the way. This gives us time to repent so He can begin to turn the situation around. *God always gives grace before calamity comes.*

My philosophy is that you can't do anything yourself. Your people have to do it.
— Beth Prichard

Treating Employees With Honor

Just because an employer is a Christian doesn't necessarily mean they treat their employees right. In fact, Christian bosses can become just as greedy as unbelievers. In the following passage of Scripture, James has a message of rebuke for such employers:

James 5:4-6

> Behold, the hire of the labourers who have reaped down your fields, which is of you kept back by fraud, crieth: and the cries of them which have reaped are entered into the ears of the Lord of sabaoth.
>
> Ye have lived in pleasure on the earth, and been wanton; ye have nourished your hearts, as in a day of slaughter.

Ye have condemned and killed the just;
and he doth not resist you.

James is challenging Christian businessmen who have fallen short of God's standard for fair treatment of their employees. These Christian bosses were treating their employees worse than worldly bosses treated their employees. It had become so prevalent, it reached public awareness!

James is reminding these men that Christian management has a higher standard to live up to than the world does. They are not only watched and scrutinized by believers, but by unbelievers, too. Most importantly, *they are being watched by God, Himself.*

The way bosses treat employees has always been an issue with God. Laban took advantage of Jacob and lowered his salary ten times (Genesis 31:41). He also tricked him into working seven more years for him by deceiving Jacob on his wedding day. But God saw everything that happened. He watched over Jacob and caused him to prosper greatly while Laban lost everything.

THE WAY BOSSES TREAT EMPLOYEES HAS ALWAYS BEEN AN ISSUE WITH GOD.

The Holy Spirit tells us, *"God resisteth the proud"* (1 Peter 5:5).

The Greek says, *"God sets Himself in battle array against the arrogant."* When a boss becomes arrogant and does not treat his employees fairly, God goes to war.

James says the cries of the workers have entered into the ears of the Lord of Sabaoth. The Jewish members of James' congregation knew the meaning of this Old Testament title for the Lord. This is not the Lord of Sabbath, "The Lord of Rest," but *Sabaoth*, "The Lord of Hosts." It is God's war title. In Hebrew it means, "Jehovah of Armies."

When the cries of mistreated and underpaid employees come into the ears of the Lord, He does not answer sweetly, but rises up in anger. Armies of angels stand ready to do battle against the greedy, self-centered boss.

Every business must operate within a certain

budget, but for those who have held back honestly-earned wages, this passage says to them, "God has heard the cries of the innocent and He will rise up and fight." Obviously, it's better to have God fighting *for* you than against you. God should be your *business partner* — not your business enemy!

GOD'S WORD TO BOSSES

What is God's perspective toward employees? How would your Master business partner want your hired personnel to be treated?

Colossians 4:1

> *Masters* [bosses], *give unto your servants* [employees] *that which is just* [fair] *and equal* [equitable]; *knowing that ye also have a Master in heaven.*

The example for bosses is the Lord, Himself. You, as a business owner, supervisor, or department head, should remember you have a boss over you who is always fair in the treatment of His people and always rewards them equitably.

God tells you to give your employees that which is "just." This means to *pay them fairly,* giving them the proper amount of pay for the job performed. Keep informed about what other businesses in your town are paying their workers so you will know about changes in the going rate.

> GOD TELLS YOU TO GIVE YOUR
> EMPLOYEES THAT WHICH IS
> "JUST." THIS MEANS TO *PAY
> THEM FAIRLY.*

Next, God says to give your employees that which is "equal" or equitable. Don't favor one employee over another. Equitable pay brings *security* and *stability* to the work force and *honor to the Lord.*

Many Christian bosses treat Christian employees with special favor. This is not God's plan. God sends the sun and rain on the just and the unjust (Matthew 5:45). Our Father wants Christian bosses to treat all employees the same. Raises, promotions, and bonuses should be given to all who deserve them. Any pay differences should be solely the result of proven integrity and increased performance. Paul tells bosses, *"...knowing that your Master* [boss] *also is in heaven; neither is there respect of persons* [partiality] *with him"* (Ephesians 6:9).

In the workplace, the practice of equality can be a witness to the unbeliever of the fairness and goodness of God. Rather than view unbelievers as outsiders who threaten our faith and the stability of our company, we can "love" them into the kingdom of God by fairness and equal treatment. Bosses, *how you treat your employees is a witness to them of how our heavenly Father treats His family.*

TRADING PLACES

A good test for any boss is to put himself in his employees' place. Ask yourself a question: "How well could I live on what my employees make?"

Managers often become accustomed to living on their level of income and ignore the cries of their workers. Groceries, rent, car payments, and child care are difficult enough on manager's pay. How would you like to make ends meet on half your income? Children's clothes, food, and gasoline cost the same for an office manager and his administrative staff as it does for you, Mr. or Ms. Business Owner!

Perhaps that new budget you are preparing should allow more room for raises and bonuses. The other projects for which you've set money aside may seem less important when compared to the benefits of having a happy and productive work force.

Aren't you glad God has budgeted your needs and your desires into His eternal plan? How would you feel if you asked God for something and were told He couldn't do it because the riches of heaven were being used to build new mansions for the eternal city?

> ## AREN'T YOU GLAD GOD HAS BUDGETED YOUR NEEDS AND YOUR DESIRES INTO HIS ETERNAL PLAN?

If you are the apple (treasure) of God's eye, shouldn't your employees be the apple of your eye?

SECURE BOSSES MAKE
SECURE EMPLOYEES

Ephesians 6:9:

> *And, ye masters* [bosses], *do the same things* [give equal treatment] *unto them* [employees], *forbearing threatening: knowing that your Master also is in heaven.*

This passage tells us what we have already heard in other passages, but adds something else very important: *Bosses should forbear threatening.* Paul is telling the Christian business owners and managers not to be bullies over their employees.

Many equate the term "boss" with "tyrant." The picture of the coach chewing out his team to spur them on to win the game often carries over into the marketplace and produces bosses who become cranky, bullying coaches. This management style gives everyone the idea that the boss is smart and the employees are stupid. Yet employees will always perform better when treated with respect and dignity. There may come times when the boss will have to pull employees back into line for taking advantage of break times and lunch hours, but a word to the wise is always better than a lecture to the ignorant.

Some employers feel it is always necessary to remind the employees who is the boss. But isn't this obvious? Don't you think your employee knew who the boss was when they were hired? Aren't they reminded every morning when they drive past your parking place right next to the front door? They see your name and title on your door each day. It is an insult for them to be told of your position so often.

A boss who often reminds his employees of his position is insecure. He demands obedience rather than cooperation. He needs the assurance each day from those around him that he is boss. *Insecure bosses produce insecure employees.* These are the types of managers who are despised and made light of when they are absent. An organization headed by an insecure boss is filled with mistrust: Employees don't trust the boss and the boss doesn't trust the employees.

A BOSS WHO OFTEN REMINDS HIS EMPLOYEES OF HIS POSITION IS INSECURE. HE DEMANDS OBEDIENCE RATHER THAN COOPERATION.

Ephesians 6:9 tells us the Lord is our example. How would you feel if the Lord reminded you each day that He is God and you are not? (That would certainly be a lesson in the obvious!) God is secure in His position and encourages us each day to be secure in ours.

Security builds trust. We trust God, and, even more importantly, we know God trusts us. It is a pleasure to be a child of God and cooperate with Him in the daily operation of His kingdom.

As goes leadership, so go the followers. *A secure boss makes for secure employees, and an organization filled with mutual trust cannot be easily divided or destroyed.* As you build trust, you will discover a new dimension of strength in your business.

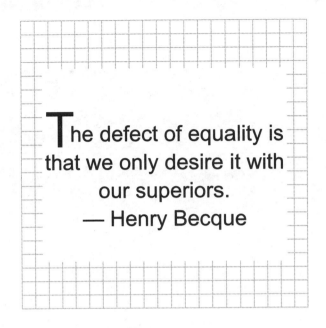

The defect of equality is that we only desire it with our superiors.

— Henry Becque

Be An Employee Of Integrity

I f asked the question, "Why do you work?" most believers would answer, "So we can have food on our table." However, according to the following verse, this is not God's reason for us to have jobs.

Ephesians 4:28

Let him that stole steal no more: but rather let him labour, working with his hands the thing which is good, that he may have to give to him that needeth.

This verse tells us Christians have jobs so they can give to those in need. In other words, *we work to expand the kingdom of God.* The employee, the boss, and the business itself are God's means of generating income in the earth to win souls, minister to the suffering, and disciple believers into mature Christians.

BE A LABORER, NOT A THIEF!

There are many verses in both the Old and New Testaments written to employees about their attitudes and productivity on the job. God's standards of integrity aren't limited to bosses, but extend to employees as well.

There are Christians today who don't want to work, yet they expect God to supply all their needs. Instead of accepting responsibility and looking for a job, they expect others to give them groceries and other provisions. They see these gifts as an answer to their "prayers of faith."

Let there be no misunderstanding about this issue: If you are capable of working, yet continue to live off handouts from other people, you are stealing. This verse in Ephesians tells us, *"Let him that stole steal no more...."* When we get a job, we quit stealing. So what should we do? Get a job!

IF YOU ARE CAPABLE OF WORKING, YET CONTINUE TO LIVE OFF HANDOUTS FROM OTHER PEOPLE, YOU ARE STEALING.

Often people want to sit back and wait for God to drop riches on them. They think this should be the normal Christian way of life. This practice is not only impractical, it is unscriptural. God has never advocated laziness in His Word.

Over the years, people have frequently come to me saying they are not able to pay all their bills. They have cut back as much as possible and still are not making it. They ask me what to do. My answer is, "Get a better job, or get another job."

Paul had to get a job. When his finances ran out, he didn't send a letter to all the churches he had started and ask for a special offering. He determined not to be a burden to anyone — and God blessed him. Because he was willing to take outside work, God put a burden on the hearts of the Macedonians to send him a love offering (see 2 Corinthians 11:9).

WHERE DO I START?

We have all heard someone say, "I just can't find a job." They tell us they have looked everywhere but just can't find anything suitable. The newspapers may be full of job opportunities, and "help wanted" signs may be everywhere but somehow these people can't find work.

Many believers are unable to find jobs because they believe certain jobs are beneath their dignity. They want to find a high-level job making a substantial salary, but they are not willing to start by making hamburgers, cleaning offices, or working at a convenience store.

If we choose to do nothing, what can God bless? He has promised to bless *all the works of our hands.* But if we choose not to work, we will have nothing to give Him that He can multiply back to us. He cannot promote us if we are inactive.

Ephesians 4:28 tells us not only to work with our hands, but the original language actually says to *work to the point of sweating!* God's plan is for believers to start small and then, later on, be promoted into positions of supervision and management. Some may even move beyond those positions to start their own businesses. The place to start, however, is with physical labor — to the point of sweating.

God's first priority is not so much to find each of us a great position, but for us to have the right attitude. He wants to see if we will be found faithful, if we will humble ourselves by having a servant's attitude and do the most menial tasks. At the right time, He will promote us (1 Peter 5:6).

RESPECT FOR THE BOSS

1 Peter 2:18,19,21

> *Servants, be subject to your masters with all fear; not only to the good and gentle, but also to the froward.*

> *For this is thankworthy, if a man for conscience toward God endure grief, suffering wrongfully....*

> *For even hereunto were ye called: because Christ also suffered for us, leaving us an example, that ye should follow his steps.*

In modern English, this verse would read, *"Employees, be submissive and respectful to your bosses, not only to the good and gentle ones, but also to the unreasonable and the unjust ones."*

Many believers work for unreasonable and unjust bosses. Any dealings with them are rarely the highlight of the workday. Many dream of working for a Christian boss, but they fail to realize that all Christians are not wonderful bosses either. Even a Christian boss can be unreasonable and unjust. They should not be but often are.

However, this verse does not give us license to work diligently for the good and gentle, and carelessly for the unreasonable and unjust. We are to give the same good day's work to both, because we owe it to them. This is part of our witness for the Lord. *How we work for our employer is a portion of the gospel we are called to preach.*

Jesus left us the greatest example of how we are to respond to the unreasonable and unjust. When He was crucified, He went before men who falsely accused Him and beat Him wrongfully. Jesus gave the matter over to the Father God, who eventually raised Him up to rule over all men.

If you are working for a manager who wrongfully accuses you, loads you down with unreasonable amounts of work, or treats you unjustly in front of others, put your trust in the same God who raised Jesus from the dead. Your day of promotion will come. God will see to it that you are promoted, either on this job or to another business. It may seem impossible at the moment, but so did the situation with the Lord Jesus. The Lord of Sabaoth will fight for you!

RESPECTING PEOPLE AND PROPERTY

Titus 2:9,10

> *Exhort servants* [employees] *to be obedient unto their own masters* [bosses], *and to please them well in all things; not answering again;*

> *Not purloining* [pilfering], *but shewing all good fildelity; that they may adorn the*

doctrine of God our Saviour in all things.

These two verses are directed toward employees' attitudes about bosses and business property. Verse nine tells us that even if we don't agree with our boss, we have no right to talk back to him. You may want to tell your boss that you disagree, but there is a time, a place, and a way of doing it which will bring glory to the Lord. Talking back shows great disrespect for your boss, and it is rebellious. You may think it will help your reputation with the other employees, but talking back rarely makes you look good to anyone.

Another problem employees face is the natural tendency to lose respect for a boss they have worked under for many years. After awhile, they know all the faults of their boss and often feel they could run the company more efficiently themselves. This may be true, but the fact remains, they are still the employee, not the boss. We are not only to respect the smart bosses but the inadequate ones as well. When you know what the Word of God has to say, you will be able to respect the boss whether anyone else does or not, *because you are respecting the position* the boss holds and not the the individual who holds the position.

...YOU ARE RESPECTING THE POSITION THE BOSS HOLDS AND NOT THE THE INDIVIDUAL WHO HOLDS THE POSITION.

Another common pitfall in working for a company several years is a lack of respect for business property. Titus is told to warn the working members of his congregation not to *purloin*. This is an old English word for *pilfering* or *petty theft*.

Just because you have worked for a company for several years does not give you the right to take property from the company no matter how small it may seem. The company paid good money for the screwdrivers, switches, nuts and bolts, ink pens, pencils, rubber bands, and paper you have taken home. No matter what you think, they do not owe you these things, and years on the job doesn't give you the right to steal from your employer.

STEALING TIME

One of the most subtle ways to pilfer from a company is to steal time. This can be easily accomplished by coming in a few minutes late, taking longer breaks and lunch hours, and being ready to leave a few minutes before quitting time. A person who is chronically late is a thief to his company.

You can also be a petty thief of time by not working as hard as you can when you are on your job.

Ephesians 6:5,6

> *Servants, be obedient to them that are your masters according to the flesh, with fear and trembling, in singleness of your heart, as unto Christ;*
>
> *Not with eyeservice, as men pleasers; but as the servants of Christ, doing the will of God from the heart.*

Paul admonishes the working saints at Ephesus to put maximum effort into their job *"with singleness of heart, as unto Christ."* Ultimately, a Christian works for One Boss, the Lord Jesus. He is always present when you come in late and when you leave early. He never is gone from the room: He is ever present and knows the effort you excercise on your job.

Paul also tells the believers not to work with "eyeservice." Eyeservice employees work when the boss is looking and don't work when he is absent. They are stealing something which cannot be returned. If someone takes pens, rubber bands, screwdrivers, etc., they can bring them back. However, time stolen from the company cannot be replaced. A Christian who is aware of the Lord's presence at all times will work hard for the company and be a model employee.

EYESERVICE EMPLOYEES WORK
WHEN THE BOSS IS LOOKING AND
DON'T WORK WHEN HE
IS ABSENT.

CHOOSING A CAREER

Many members of the congregation ask me about choosing a career in life.

"Pastor," they say, "I just don't know what to do in life. I come to church, I pray, I honor God in giving, and I read the Word, but I just don't have a leading from the Lord for a profession."

I ask them, "What do you *want* to do?"

They often reply, "Oh, Pastor, I don't think it would be right to do what I *want* to do. I want to do what God wants for my life."

When I tell them God wants them to do what they want to do, they are usually surprised. You see, the desires which are in our hearts are God-given (Psalm 37:4). God not only grants the desires we have in our hearts, He also places those desires. If you are endeavoring to follow God and are seeking Him, your career desire is probably from God.

So, I ask them again, "What would you *like* to do?"

"Well, Pastor, I would like to build houses."

I tell them, "So, go build houses."

David told us in Psalm 1:3 that if a man puts God first, *"..whatsoever he doeth shall prosper."* If God has something else for you to do, He will tell you as

He finds you faithfully doing what you desire to do. Follow your desires, work with integrity, and God will surely prosper you!

Hiding your head in the
sand isn't the best way to
hold your end up.
— Unknown

Keeping Your Partnership Unlimited

Sowing good seeds into your business or job today will ensure its success tomorrow and for generations to come. God would love to make your business an enduring enterprise. In fact, He wants this even more than you do. He would like to see your business continue to be successful for many years to come so your children can continue to use the profits to spread the gospel.

IMPORTANT SCRIPTURAL PRINCIPLES TO FOLLOW

If you desire to keep your business partnership unlimited, here are a few points to consider:

1.   Dedicate your business to the Lord.

It is not your business but His. He owns

everything anyway (Psalm 50:10-12). He only asks you to be a wise steward over His possessions. If God truly is your business partner, then dedicate it to Him. This involves a daily study of the Word of God. Your office manual should be the Bible. Reading this manual will ensure you unlimited resources, unlimited wisdom, and an unlimited partnership.

2.   Pray daily over the business.

One of the most important reasons why businesses fail is a lack of communication. There are seminars given daily across this country teaching the importance of communications from the boss to the employee, from the employee to the boss, and from employee to employee. All of this is good, but the most important piece of communication is left out, the communication from God to the owner.

If God will lead, guide, direct, protect, heal, forgive, and prosper you as an individual, He will do it for your business as well.   Pray over purchases, sales, investments, hiring, expansion, and the host of other concerns you face daily in business. An ounce of prayer is worth a pound of repentance!

IF GOD WILL LEAD, GUIDE,
DIRECT, PROTECT, HEAL,
FORGIVE, AND PROSPER YOU
AS AN INDIVIDUAL, HE WILL DO IT
FOR YOUR BUSINESS AS WELL.

If "hindsight is 20/20," you can already see the many times you should have prayed. You realize now that you were not as smart in the past as you thought you were. What makes you believe you have become smarter? Take it for granted, you still are not as smart as God. Turn those future plans over to the Lord and pray for wisdom. God has already told us He will give wisdom to us abundantly (James 1:5).

3.   Quit looking for quick riches.

Proverbs 23:5

Wilt thou set thine eyes upon that which is

not? For riches certainly make themselves wings; they fly away as an eagle toward heaven.

This verse tells us that overnight riches take on overnight wings. Remember, God blesses your business the same way He blesses you. Your business will *"prosper and be in health even as thy soul prospereth"* (3 John 2). You did not understand the whole realm of Christian doctrine the day after you were saved, and neither will your riches come in this way.

There is always progression in the kingdom of God. It is *"first the blade, then the ear, after that the full corn in the ear"* (Mark 4:28). It is *"some thirtyfold, some sixty, and some an hundred"* (Mark 4:20), and *"that good, and acceptable, and perfect, will of God"* (Romans 12:2).

4. Don't enter into a business relationship with an unbeliever.

    Paul instructs us in 2 Corinthians 6:14 not to

be unequally yoked together with unbelievers. Although this verse is usually applied to marriages, it was primarily directed to the businessmen of Corinth. You should not be joined to an unbelieving partner. You should go into partnership with a mature believer who possesses the same vision and convictions you do.

It is easy to excuse this principle when you find someone interested in partnership who has capital to put into the business. You may feel you need to compromise on this point because you need this person's money to get your business going.

You will find that the secret to success in business is not capital, but *integrity*. You do not lack money, you lack ideas. Ideas ultimately come from the Lord. When you and your business partner are both seeking the perfect will of God, the ideas will come, the money will be generated, and the business will prosper. Remember, true prosperity for you and your business does not begin with money; *it begins with a relationship with the Lord.*

...THE SECRET TO SUCCESS IN BUSINESS IS NOT CAPITAL, BUT INTEGRITY

5. Hire spiritually mature believers as employees.

    Employees are junior partners in your business. Most of the sins listed in the New Testament are sins of believers, not unbelievers! Since Christians can often steal, cheat, and lie better than sinners, screen your applicants and be sensitive to the leading of the Holy Spirit as well as to their qualifications. It would be good to contact their church and find out about their faithfulness to attend, volunteer, and give into the work of the Lord.

    You do not have to have the type of employee problems experienced by the world. God has a better plan for the business in which He is a partner. Unlimited partnerships have integrity from the head office to the maintenance department.

6. Be a giver from your business.

If *"the liberal soul shall be made fat [prosperous]"* (Proverbs 11:25), then so will the *liberal business.* Don't hide behind the excuses of many businessmen: "My assets are not liquid." Give when the transaction is first completed. Don't wait for the profits to be invested before thinking of the Lord. The Bible says, *"Honor the Lord...with the firstfruits of all thine increase"* (Proverbs 3:9). God has never blessed anyone, whether an individual or a business, for leftover scraps.

God always blesses us with His firstfruits. He gave us Jesus the Firstfruits and daily loads us with benefits — the best from heaven. Why shouldn't we give back to God in the same way?

When you line up your business practices with the Word of God, you will see prosperity Scriptures come to pass in the daily operations of your company. Giving to the work of the Lord will become a great joy and pleasure to you. More than that, you will be rewarded throughout eternity for the ministry your finances made possible and for the lives that were changed because of your generosity and your Unlimited Partnership with God.

Failure is fertilizer,
the stuff from which
successes grow.

— Unknown

Winning with Integrity

THERE IS SOMETHING BETTER THAN MONEY

Proverbs 11:4:

Riches profit not in the day of wrath: but righteousness (integrity) delivers from death.

The old expression Money can't buy everything is true. When you are in real trouble, you cannot always buy your way out. The Holy Spirit does not necessarily protect the Christian with money, but He does protect the one with integrity. As this verse tells us, integrity can save your life.

What is integrity? The dictionary definition is

moral uprightness, a principled life, honesty. There is little integrity in the world today and sadly, not enough of it in the Christian community. When a person operates in integrity, it causes them to stand out.

INTEGRITY CAN SAVE YOUR LIFE.

Integrity can save you large sums of money in advertising. Integrity spreads your good name and reputation faster than any television, radio, newspaper or even the internet. Your business can operate and thrive when based on and operated in integrity. You do not have to announce you are a business of integrity, paint a fish on the door, or say "Praise the Lord" every other sentence. Your integrity will speak for itself.

Integrity is better than money. Without it, you may be unable to obtain money or you may obtain money, but will be unable keep your riches. Integrity is the foundation for success in both your spiritual life and your business life. Integrity insures that God will continue to be your Unlimited Partner.

GOD, YOURSELF AND OTHERS

Adam began his business of working and protecting the garden with only God and himself. Integrity first begins with your accountability to God. You may be able to hide your actions from others, but God sees everything you do (Hebrews 4:13). When you realize this, you understand your Unlimited Partner is a witness to every business transaction and promise you make.

Secondly, integrity is directed toward yourself. Shakespeare said, "To your own self be true." Even if you do not think God sees everything you do, YOU DO! You may be able to cheat someone in your business dealings and never see them again, but you have to go home with yourself every time. You have to live with yourself and your conscience. A lack of integrity will kill you. If nothing else, it will keep you from sleeping at night wondering if the customer found your misdeed. One angry, cheated client can destroy your reputation in the community.

A LACK OF INTEGRITY
WILL KILL YOU

Thirdly, your integrity is with others. Jesus died for people because He loves them (John 3:16). His love in our heart is spread to others by the power of the Holy Spirit (Romans 5:5). Perhaps you will think twice about lying to a customer when you realize they are a person Jesus died for. If they are a Christian, you will spend eternity in heaven with them. What if your mansion is next door to theirs forever? It will be nice to look across the fence at them and remember you treated them with integrity.

GOD IS HONEST AND HE
LOVES HONESTY

Proverbs 11:1:

A false balance is an abomination to the Lord: but a just weight is his delight.

A just balance is a synonym for integrity of the heart. In the ancient world, the business owner would weigh the purchase on a set of scales. A dishonest business owner would put false weights on the scales to tip the profits more in his favor. God has many warnings against this practice (Leviticus 19:35, Deuteronomy 25:13-15).

Proverbs 16:11:

A just weight and balance are the Lord's. all the weights of the bag are his work.

Here is a great way to prosper: BE HONEST. God, your Unlimited Partner, will supernaturally work for you and bless you. When you are honest, God causes the prosperity to come to you. He blesses the work of your hand

HERE IS A GREAT WAY TO PROSPER: BE HONEST

Without God's help, you are left to try to bless yourself. I would rather have God's help than try to do it myself.

INTEGRITY GIVES GUIDANCE

Proverbs 11:3, 5:

The integrity of the upright shall guide them: but the perverseness (lies) of the

transgressors shall destroy them.

The righteousness of the perfect shall direct his way:

Did you know it is possible to have supernatural guidance without searching out scripture or uttering a prayer? If you are a person who strives to walk in honesty, your integrity will be a guide to you. You are not led by the Wall Street Journal, only informed by it. You are led by your integrity.

You are either being led by integrity or greed. Greed will bring you guilt, sorrow, and eventually destruction. Integrity will bring you joy, peace, spiritual stability and maturity.

Psalm 25:21:

Let integrity and uprightness preserve me; for I wait on you.

Proverbs 13:6:

Righteousness sustains him that is upright in the way: but wickedness overthrows the sinner.

Finally, when you walk in integrity, you have no fear of God's scrutiny in your life. You do not mind that your Great Business Partner looks over your shoulder every time you make a business deal. You even invite His heavenly personal and business audits.

Job 31:6:

> Let me be weighted in an even (accurate) balance, that God may know my integrity.

Psalm 26:1:

> Judge me O Lord; for I have walked in my integrity:

A CONFESSION TO
START YOUR DAY

I have put this section into a confession you can quote at the beginning of each day. Before each business transaction, I pray it will cause you to think of God's desire for you to reflect His character to others.

Confession:

I choose this day to walk in integrity in my dealings with others. My balances will be accurate and my heart right before God and men. The Lord hates cheating but delights in honesty. I will have a reputation of honesty before God, my family and the world. As I deal in integrity, God will work for me and bring blessings to me. Integrity will be my guide, leading me to do what is honorable. Righteousness and honesty will deliver and preserve me from the traps others fall into. God has promised me, if I would be a person of integrity, I would live long on the earth and enjoy the land God has given me.

BOOKS BY BOB YANDIAN

The Fullness of the Spirit
Decently and In Order
Let Your Light Shine
You Have a Ministry
Spirit Controlled Life
One Nation Under God
One Flesh
Leadership Secrets of David the King
From Just Enough to Overflowing
Unlimited Partnership
Grace: From Here to Eternity
Understanding the End Times
Back in the Race
Fellowshipping with God
Righteousness: God's Gift to You
Forever Changed
Ephesians
Proverbs
Joel
Resurrection
God's Word to Pastors
Philippians Notes
Colossians Notes
James Notes

HOW TO CONTACT
BOB YANDIAN MINISTRIES

Email:
bym@gracetulsa.com

Phone:
1-800-284-0595
Local: (918) 250-2207

Fax:
(918) 317-5025

Mailing Address:
Bob Yandian Ministries
PO Box 55236
Tulsa, OK 74155

Website:
bobyandian.com